MW01515220

Why We Crave Love

The Untold Truth

Olympia Walker

Why We Crave Love

Scriptures taken from The Holy Bible, the King James Version. Copyright ©

"Scripture taken from the New King James Version. Copyright © 1982 by Thomas Nelson, Inc.

Used by permission. All rights reserved."

Scripture quotations marked NLT are taken from the Holy Bible, New Living Translation, copyright 1996, 2004. Used by permission of Tyndale House Publishers, Inc., Wheaton, Illinois 60189. All rights reserved.

Cover Design: Wow Publishing,

P.O. Box 1585

Copperas Cove, Texas 76522

www.wordsofwisdompublishing@gmail.com

ISBN-10: 0-9977161-0-X

ISBN-13: 978-0-9977161-0-8

Editor: Felicia L. Chisholm

Contact Information:

Mstruth97@hotmail.com

Facebook: Felicia L. Chisholm

LinkedIn: Felicia Chisholm

DEDICATION

I would like to dedicate "Why We Crave Love" to everyone who has been broken, hurt, abused (physically, emotionally, and mentally), manipulated, deceived, betrayed, and abandoned due to the lack of understanding on what love truly is.

My Prayer for Readers

Most Gracious Heavenly Father,

I come to you praying that You will give each person reading this book a clear understanding of who You are. Show them how important it is to have a personal relationship with Your Son Jesus Christ. Allow Your Holy Spirit to teach each reader to "Trust in the Lord with all their hearts, And lean not to their own understanding; In all their ways acknowledge You and You shall direct their path." Open up their heart to receive what You would have for them to receive. Allow them to find a deep love for You, so they will no longer have to search for love in people, money, jobs/careers, and material things. Father, I ask this prayer in Your Darling Son Jesus Christ name.

WHY WE CRAVE LOVE

TABLE OF CONTENTS

ACKNOWLEDGMENTS

I would like to give all the praise, glory and honor to God for giving me the vision to write this book because if it had not been for Him, I probably would not have had the courage to write it.

To my husband, children, grandchildren and brother, I love you all very much.

Preface

This book was not written to replace or interpret the Bible. However, the purpose of this book is to focus on real life issues that will lead you directly to the scripture. My prayer is that the contents of this book will inspire readers to read the word of God, develop a personal relationship with God, repent of their sins, apply the word of God to their life, be obedient to the word of God, accept Jesus Christ as their Lord and Savior, and to live a life that is totally souled out to God in every area of their life.

If you are looking to grow spiritually, enhance your knowledge and understanding of God, find your true love, live a better life, be obedient, and develop a personal relationship with God, then this book is for you. *"Why We Crave Love"* is filled with everything you need to start you on your way to live the way God requires us to live. Once you finish reading this book, you will know the true essence of love. You will no longer have to look for love in all the wrong places, because the love your soul is really longing for is the love that only God can give.

Writing this book was very difficult for me, but I had to realize that my life does not belong to me; it belongs to the Lord. My life has nothing to do with how I feel or think; it's about doing things God's way. Often times, we get caught up in trying to do things our way. Then, when things don't work out for us the way we think it should, we blame or question God. If the truth be told, nine times out of ten, God was nowhere in the planning process of the decision(s) we have made. When it comes to God, we treat Him as if we are playing a game of monopoly and He is our get out of jail free card. The only time we call on Him is when things are not going the way we think it should go or if we are in trouble. Then, as so as God gets us out of our mess, we have the audacity to turn right back around and do the same thing over and over again. We think we can play "Let's Make a Deal" with Him, but what we fail to realize is God knows the very intent of our heart. He knows when and if we are sincere.

As you read this book take an inward look at yourself and where you are in Jesus Christ. If you are ready for a life-changing experience, then *Why We Crave Love* will be the beginning of your new life in Jesus Christ.

Chapter 1

"Don't Fool Yourself"

"And the Lord God said, It is not good that the man should be alone, I will make him an help meet for him. And the rib, which the Lord God had taken from man, made he a woman, and brought her unto the man" *(KJV, Gen. 2.18&22).*

Time and time again I've heard people say, "I'm never dating or getting married again," but then they turn around and commit fornication and/or adultery. Now, that is the craziest thing I've ever heard (well, it's not the craziest thing, but you get my point). You mean to tell me that you would go from something that God honors and approves of (marriage), to something He hates (sin)? Marriage is ordained by God and it honors Him. God does not honor shacking-up, fornication or adultery. I don't care if they are separated or in the process of getting divorced, it does not honor nor please God. Do not fall for the tricks of the enemy just because it sounds good. And if you are in that situation right now, run and don't look back. Get out of there now!

If the truth be told, the only reason why people say things like, "I'm not dating or getting married again" is because they have been hurt at some point or another in their life. I know what you are thinking: "But you don't know what I've been through." Right? Well, I've been there and said that too; but, the only time I made that statement was because I had been hurt. Come on though, be honest with yourself. You are only speaking from an emotional point right now because you have been hurt or maybe you are hurting as you read this book. Think back to when you were a kid learning how to ride your brand-new bike. Before you mastered the concept of riding your bike, you fell. Right? You may have even gotten a few scrapes and bruises, but did you give up? No, you got up and kept trying. Before you knew it, you were riding your bike without falling.

Well, sometimes relationships are like that too. Yeah, you may get a few scrapes and bruises emotionally, and maybe even physically, or maybe the person you loved passed away, but that is no reason to give up on love. I know some of you are still shaking your head saying, "You just don't understand." I understand that you may have lost someone close to you due to death or maybe someone has hurt you. You swore to yourself that you would never love again, right? Well, again, I've been there and said that too. Let me share something with you. I have been through bad relationship after bad relationship. I even lost someone I was dating due to death and I've said those same words, "I'm never dating again." Who was I kidding? That only last for a moment. Although it took me some time to get over the hurt and pain from losing someone I loved, I found myself in another relationship. It wasn't like I was out there looking to get involved in another relationship, but it happened.

When it comes to our life, we think we know best- especially in relationships. We tend to jump into relationships because of looks, money, pregnancy, and sex, not knowing that we might be headed down the road of getting hurt. Why? Because we tend to get caught up in the wrong things when it comes to being in a relationship. We don't even think to ask God to show us what's best for us or if we should be in that relationship in the first place. Then, the moment we get hurt we say, "Why me God?" I was guilty of that too! We think we know what's best and try to plan our lives, then we wonder why our lives are a mess. Do we really know what's best for us when it comes to relationships? No, if we did, we wouldn't find ourselves in one bad relationship after another.

All too often, we like to place blame on the other person when we get hurt in relationships. Truth be told, we knew we shouldn't have been in that relationship from the start. In Proverbs 20:24 (NKJV) it says, "A man's steps are of the Lord; How then can a man understand his own way?" Man is non-gendered in that Proverb. God is the only one who knows what's best for us. After all, God created mankind, so He knows us better than we know ourselves. He knew us when we were yet in our mother's womb. He knows our comings and our goings. We need to ask ourselves, are we above God?

4

Oh, we may not say it with our mouths, but like the old saying goes, "Actions speaks louder than words." What are your actions saying?

Listen, don't fool yourself into thinking you don't need anybody, nor am I suggesting you do, but, we need to ask God what is His will for our lives in everything we do before we mess things up. Genesis 1:1 KJV says, "In the beginning after God created the heavens and the earth." Verse 26a goes on to say, "And God said, Let us make man in our image, after our likeness:" Verse 27 also tells us, "So God created man in his own image, in the image of God created he him; male and female created he them." Okay, here comes the good part! Gen. 2:20 says, "And Adam gave names to all cattle, and to the fowl of the air, and to every beast of the field; but for Adam there was not found a help meet for him." You know the rest of the story. So, if God created a help meet for Adam, are we not descendants of him? Is Adam above us? God has someone out there especially for you (if you are single).

Now, don't get me wrong; when it comes to relationships, every day is not going to be a bed of roses-whether dating or married, but when we place God first in everything we say and do, He will show us how to handle anything - even when it comes to relationships. When we try to handle things our way, we mess it up, and we want God to fix our mess. We got a lot of nerves, huh? Don't let your circumstance dictate your life; let God dictate your circumstance(s). Whatever the problem is, give it to God and He will work it out for your good, no matter what the result is. Okay, I know what you are thinking! Giving things over to God is easier said than done, right? Well, if we really trust God like we claim to, giving things over to Him will be easy. However, the truth of the matter is we really don't trust God. Why? Because we don't know Him. Oh, we say we know Him, but do we really? Truthfully, we really don't know God personally for ourselves. We only know of Him based on what we have heard someone else say because it sounds good. We only want God to bless us with material possessions and a husband or wife, but we don't want to trust Him with our lives. Nor do we want a relationship with Him. Ask me how I know! I know because if we trust God with our life, it would show up in our actions. Again, actions speak louder than words. What are your actions saying?

Okay, for those of you who don't believe that actions speak louder than words, wait until the next trial, storm, disappointment, hurt or whatever happens in your life and see how you will react. What you say or how you respond will tell if you really know and trust God. Take it from me, I've definitely been there more than once. I have learned a lot in my life. And one of those things I've learned is, what we say doesn't really matter, it's our actions that counts. We say we trust God and have prayed about a situation and have given the problem to Him, but we still have our hand in it. We try to fix the problem ourselves instead of trusting God to work it out. I have been guilty of that before and God is still yet working on me with that. "But those who wait on the Lord shall renew their strength; they shall mount up with wings like eagles, they shall run and not be weary, they shall walk and not faint" (NKJV, Isaiah 40:31). Wait on God! All I am trying to say is keep your focus on The Lord. He knows what you need and don't need. So, say it with me, I am not above God and He knows what's best for me. Don't you feel much better? I know I do with just the thought of knowing that God loves me so much that He has my best interest at heart.

7

The more time you spend getting to know God the easier it will be to trust Him. To know God is to spend time in His word getting to know who He is and how to obey Him. Stop going by what you've heard someone say just because it sounds biblical. Get to know Jesus Christ for yourself. He wants a relationship with you. After all, He created us for Himself. Remember that so called friend you thought you had? When you first met that person you spent time with them before you trusted them with your business, right? As time went by, your friendship grew closer and closer. Before you knew it, you began to trust that person; but, little did you know one day that person would betray your trust. Well, God is not like man (non-gendered). He will never betray your trust. Aren't you glad about that?

"Trust in the Lord with all your heart, And lean not on your own understanding; In all your ways acknowledge Him, And He shall direct your paths" (NKJV, Prov. 3.5&6).

If we could only get that scripture right, our lives would be less complicated. God will work every situation out in your life if you would just trust Him and surrender to

His will. Isaiah 55:8-9 (KJV) tells us, "For
my thoughts are not your thoughts, neither
are your ways my ways, saith the Lord. For
as the heavens are higher than the earth, so
are my ways higher than your ways, and my
thoughts than your thoughts." Now, that is
plain and clear! Just in case you still don't
get it, let me break it down for you. We
cannot begin to be on the same level as the
Lord. See, when we try to handle situations
on our own or make plans without consulting
Him first, we are saying we are above God.
Let's look at verse 9 again. It says, "For as
the heavens are higher than the earth, so are
my ways higher than your ways, and my
thoughts than your thoughts." Wow! That
should have blessed you! Think about it!
The Lord knows <u>EVERYTHING!</u> He does not
operate like we do. Aren't you glad about
that? I know I am! Don't fool yourself into
thinking that you do not need a man (ladies)
or a woman (men) just because you had a
troubled relationship(s)/marriage in the
past. In the beginning, God saw the need for
<u>man</u> not to be alone so He created a <u>woman</u>
for him (we will deal with that in the next
chapter). God joined the two together and
they became one. And ladies, don't settle for
being somebody's bed warmer, shacking
partner, special friend, friend with benefits,

late night creep, or the other woman. Listen, if you don't respect yourself, how can you expect for him to respect you? If he doesn't respect you, he will use you up, and then when he is tired of you he will move to someone else. That's if he is not already seeing you and someone else. Ladies, love and respect yourself, because if you don't, how do you expect someone else to?

Now, don't think for one second that you are the only one who has been or is in this situation. Trust me, you are not alone! The problem is no one wants to be honest on where they have been because they are afraid of what people might say or think about them. I was once ignorant and in the same situation myself, but glory be to God that He opened my eyes to who His Son is and how He died for my sins. Now here's the blessing in knowing that Jesus Christ died for our sins. Once we ask for forgiveness for our sins and turn away from them, we are no longer guilty or in bondage of those sins. Isn't that a blessing? For me, that brings joy to my soul.

You will not be sorry to have gotten to know God for yourself. After all, you've tried things your way and your life hasn't seemed to have gotten any better. Trust me, I've been down that same road many times and the more I stayed on it, the worst things were. So, I caution you! If your life is headed down that highway called Hot Mess, take the nearest exit to Trust God Boulevard, where He will give you direction to your destination. Ask yourself this question. What do you have to lose? Trust me, with God on your side, you stand to gain far more than this world could ever offer. So, please do not fool yourself into thinking you know what's best for your life. Only God Himself knows what's best for you. "For I know the thoughts that I think toward you, saith the Lord, thoughts of peace, and not of evil, to give you an expected end" (KJV, Jeremiah 29:11).

Chapter 2

"Take Your Blinders Off"

"Now the serpent was more subtle than any beast of the field which the Lord God had made" (KJV, Gen. 3:1a).

When God created Eve for Adam in Genesis, that union represented a covenant marriage between a man and a woman. It not only represents the marriage between a man and a woman, but it represents the marriage covenant between Christ and the Church (His bride). Many people have not gotten this concept yet. It seems no one values the marriage covenant that God established in the beginning. Marriage is honorable in the eyesight of God, but men and women have perverted the institution of marriage. The world would cause you to believe that it's okay for women to marry women and men to marry men. However, God did not create marriage to be defiled in that manner. Also, He did not create it for those who commit adultery either. Genesis 2:24 (KJV) states, "Therefore shall a <u>man</u> leave his father and his mother, and shall cleave unto his <u>wife</u>: and they shall be one flesh." There shouldn't be any confusion or debate about that scripture unless you don't believe in God. How can two men or two women become one flesh? It's like putting a puzzle together; the pieces must fit in order to see the true beauty of how the puzzle should look. If the pieces of the puzzle do not fit, that means the piece does not belong there. There is nothing natural about two men or two women being intimate/married. "But the men of Sodom were wicked and sinners before the Lord exceedingly" (KJV, Genesis 13:13).

A lot of people claim to believe in God, but their actions show different. If God's word said it, then it's true. Satan knows how important the institution of marriage is and he definitely knows the purpose in which God created male and female. When God created man and woman, He did not make any mistakes. God did not create man and say, "Oops, he's supposed to be a woman." Nor did He create woman and say, "She is supposed to be a man." I am so tired of hearing people that claim to be attracted to the same sex say, "God created or made me this way." God is not the author of confusion. He did not create men to be with men and women to be with women. People twist the word of truth (God's word) to fit their own selfish, lustful desires and lifestyles. Then, they want others to believe what they say to be true. When God formed Adam out of the dust and created Eve from Adam's rib, God's creation was perfect and complete. It wasn't until sin entered the world from Adam and Eve's disobedience that caused mankind to be born in sin. Here is where I need for you to pay close attention to what I am about to say. When Adam and Eve sinned, they cursed their offspring. That means every one of their descendants would be born with a sinful nature. It is because of the fall of man (Adam and Eve) that you have those sinful, lustful desires of being with someone of the same sex. See, the Bible says that we were born in sin and shapen in iniquity; but, wait, I have some good news for you though. Jesus Christ is able to deliver you from that type of lifestyle. As a matter of fact, He has already paid the price for your sins on the cross at

Calvary. You no longer have to live your life
in bondage, enslaved by sin. God is just
waiting for you to repent of your sins and ask
Him for forgiveness. And it is that simple,
you will be forgiven of your sins. And not
only will you be forgiven of your sins, you
will no longer be held captive to sin that
leads to destruction. Now hear me out! You
CANNOT stop sinning without the Lord
giving you the strength and the will to do so.
All you have to do is ask Him for His help,
and He will help you overcome whatever
situation you are in. We cannot do anything
on our own except for what we already know
how to do, and that is sin. Outside of a
relationship with Jesus Christ, we can do
nothing. How many times have you said you
were going to stop doing something only to
find yourself doing the very thing you said
you weren't going to do? Don't feel bad. You
are not alone; I've been there too. "For all
have sinned, and come short of the glory of
God; Being justified freely by His grace
through the redemption that is in Christ
Jesus" (KJV, Romans 3.23-24). Call on the
name of Jesus. God is waiting to forgive,
deliver, help, and strengthen you.

God's word about things that are
unrighteous is plain to understand. In
Romans 1:18 (New Living Translation) it
says, "But God shows his anger from heaven

against all sinful, wicked people who suppress the truth by their wickedness." Verse 19 goes on to say, "They know the truth about God because He has made it obvious to them." Here is where the problem comes in. You either accept that the word of God is truth or reject it, because on that great Day of Judgment, there will be no more excuses for unrighteousness.

I would like to encourage you to go back and read Romans chapter 1 in its entirety in order to get a better understanding of what God is saying. Ask God to open your eyes to the truth and be prepared for what He shows you.

"Don't you realize that those who do wrong will not inherit the Kingdom of God? Don't fool yourselves. Those who indulge in sexual sin[fornication], or who worship idols, or commit adultery, or are male prostitutes, or practice homosexuality, or are thieves, or greedy people, or drunkards, or are abusive, or cheat people [extortioners]- none of these will inherit the Kingdom of God" (NLT, 1 Corin. 6.9-10).

See, no one will be exempt! Sin is sin! God hates ALL sin, but thank God for deliverance! I once had a first class, one-way ticket straight to hell and didn't even realize it. (Excuse me while I get my praise on! Hallelujah!) I used to be one of those people. Now I can speak with boldness on where God has brought me from because He has forgiven me for my sins. I am not ashamed of where I've been because there is one thing I realize: I've been set free from those sins! I know some of you may be looking down on me now, but just like Jesus Christ died for my sins and God forgave me, He can do the same for you.

"Some of you were once like that. But you were cleansed; you were made holy; you were made right with God be calling on the name of the Lord Jesus Christ and by the Spirit of our God" (NLT, 1Corinthians 6:11).

God's word said it, not me! And if the truth be told, some of you are still in sin. The only difference between me and you are shame and pride, and they won't let you admit where you once were or where you may still be. Shame and pride had me bound for many years, until I learned what God had to say concerning who I am. "As it is written: There is none righteous, no, not one; There is none who understands; There is none who seeks after God" (NKJV, Romans 3:10-11). You know what I have discovered? The key to true deliverance is admitting when you are wrong and what condition you are in. A friend once told me he heard a preacher say, "You are not weak when it comes to certain things; you become weak when you do those things." Wow, that was so powerful to me!

Whatever your sin is, it comes from the desires of your heart. No one does anything without first having a desire in their heart to do whatever it is they desire to do. If you think about doing something long enough, you will eventually find yourself acting upon that which you desire. Where does that desire come from? Is it already in your heart? "For out of the heart proceed evil thoughts, murders, adulteries, fornications, theft, false witness, blasphemies. These are the things which defile a man" (NKJV, Matthew 15:19-20a)." Your weakness comes when you act on something. For example, I can't say my weakness is chocolate cake if I never tasted or indulged myself in it before. What I'm trying to say is, if you don't put yourself in certain situations, you can't say those things are causing you to be weak. Meditate on that for a moment!

I heard the most disturbing news about a nine-year old boy. I guess he only plays with a lot of girls so he calls himself a tom girl. Nine years old, can you believe that? Additionally, on the news, a little boy confessed to being gay and was murdered by one of his peers. Then, there are elementary, middle, and high school kids who are experimenting in same sex relationships at school *openly.* The sad thing about this is the schools are allowing this type of behavior to take place. The teachers don't say anything to the kids when they see them walking down the halls holding hands and kissing. Come on now, what is wrong with this picture? This is what happens when you take prayer out of school!

Parents, step up and be parents and stop letting your children control you. Stop condoning this type of behavior. Don't you realize you are going to be held accountable by God for enabling your child in this type of behavior or with any other sinful acts? Parents I urge you to do an occasional drop in at your child's school to see what's going on. I've had to do it myself when my children were in school. We need to stop being so caught up in our own lives to the point that we are losing our children to society. Schools are there to educate our children, not raise them for us. Get more involved in your child/children's life, and stop trying to be their friend. My children get mad at me because I'm always on them about making the right choices. Does that mean I'm going to stop being a mother? No! Do they listen and take heed to what I say? Sometimes! Regardless, I've done my part as their mother and they can't say I didn't teach them. Who knows, one day they may listen and take heed to what I say. I'm not saying don't be their friend at all, but you have to draw the line at some point. It is hard to be a parent and a friend. If you don't draw the line between being a parent and being a friend, they will not respect you. Stay on them; they'll thank you in the end. There are numerous talk shows that have stories about out of control children/teens. Parents are scared to live in their own homes because they are afraid of their children. Who's the adult? In Proverbs 22:15 (KJV) it says, "Foolishness is bound in the heart of a child; but the rod of correction shall drive it far from him." Do you understand what is being said here? When your child/children are acting a crazy, don't be afraid to correct him or her just as God disciplines and corrects us because of His love for us.

"Withhold not correction from the child: for if thou beatest him with the rod, he shall not die. Thou shalt beat him with the rod, and shalt deliver his soul from hell" (KJV, Prov.23:13-14).

There is nothing wrong with disciplining your children. Oh, by the way, cursing is not considered discipline. Children lack stern discipline, and that may be part of the problem with children in today's society. (Calm down, I said may be!) So, if that means you have to whoop them every now and again, whoop'em. "The rod and reproof give wisdom: but a child left to himself bringeth his mother shame" (KJV, Proverbs 29:15). Society has programmed our children into thinking they're in control. Kids are fighting and divorcing their parents, calling 911 (because they are being disciplined) on their parents, and cursing their parents out. What's wrong here! Nevertheless, the same society that says, "It is okay for children to divorce their parents" is quick to lock them up and put a label on them. Something is definitely wrong with that picture, parents. Parents, it's time to start being parents and stop trying to fit in with your child/children. Proverbs 22:6 (KJV) says, "Train up a child in the way he should go: and when he is old, he will not depart from it." Parents, do you hear what God is saying?

We are not only supposed to teach our children right from wrong, but God commands us to train our children in the knowledge of His Son Jesus Christ. Now, listen, no matter how much you teach a child, they will still try to do things their way; but, it is our duty as parents to provide a solid foundation to our children, and that solid foundation is Jesus Christ. Do you not realize that everything a person needs to know about life can be found in the Bible? Every situation that we will be faced with in our life is in the Bible. Not only that, but you will find all the answers you need in order to handle whatever situation you face - the way God would have you to. If we as parents fail to bring our children up in the knowledge of Jesus Christ, then we are being disobedient to God. Here is what we fail to realize, though: God is going to hold us accountable for not training them up in the Lord.

When I was a child, I really didn't have that spiritual foundation. I mean, I can recall going to church with my great grandmother when we would go visit for the summer in Port Arthur (which wasn't too often). I can also recall a couple of times when I lived with my other grandmother on my dad's side. On other occasions, I went to church on Easter and Christmas with my cousins and their grandparents. Sometimes as kids, we would catch a bus (without our parents) to a church we knew nothing about in another city about 35-45 minutes away.

The only reason we would go to this church was because on Easter they would have a big Easter egg hunt. When we were kids, we didn't pay attention to anything the Pastor said; instead, we were either passing notes or sleep.

I was baptized at an early age because one of my cousins was getting baptized. I didn't have a clue about being baptized; I just wanted to go down in the water because it looked fun. When I was about 17, my mother tried forcing me to go to church, but by then I didn't want to hear anything about church. I started attending church at age 22, and I still didn't commit myself to God fully. Dying to self and submitting to God was a struggle for me because I wasn't studying God's word, and the only time I prayed was when I wanted God to get me out of a situation. We treat God like He is some kind of genie in a bottle. Notice I said "we," because I did it too! I thank God that He didn't give up on me, though! I was so caught up in myself and didn't realize God could have killed me in the middle of my sins. What I didn't know was, if I would have died without repenting of my sins, I would have gone to hell. And you know what, that's what I truly deserved. Thanks be to God He sent His Son to be the propitiation for my sins. Now, don't get it twisted, God is not playing with us! Proverbs 1:26 says, "I also will laugh at your calamity; I will mock when your fear cometh" (KJV). Please read verses 22-33 to get a clear picture of verse 26.

Yeah, we may think we are getting away with whatever we are doing on this side of the earth, but maybe just maybe, that is probably why we are going through some of the things we are going through. Remember, God created the heavens and the earth. When He returns we will have to give an account for everything (not some), everything we ever said and done. Okay, you don't believe me. "Behold, the Lord comes with ten thousands of His saints, to execute judgment upon all, to convict all who are ungodly among them of all their ungodly deeds which they have committed in an ungodly way, and of all the harsh things which ungodly sinners have spoken against Him" (NKJV, Jude 1 :14b-15). Hold on! Wait a minute! Let's back up for a second, because I know you may be saying, "I haven't spoken anything against God." Well, remember what I said earlier, "Actions speaks louder than words." Therefore, you don't have to actually say a word, but your actions will speak for you. Verse 16a goes on to say, "These are grumblers, complainers, walking according to their own lusts." This life is not, nor has it ever been about us; it is and has always been about God.

Chapter 3

"Don't Be Deceived"

"Be ye not unequally yoked together with unbelievers: for what fellowship hath righteousness with unrighteousness? And what communion hath light with darkness?" (KJV, 2 Corinthians 6:14).

We've all heard the saying, "Opposites attract," right? Well, that's not possible according to the Word of God. And if God's Word said it, it's true. Go back and read the scripture under the title of this chapter. Don't just read it, meditate on it and ask God to give you a clear understanding on what is being said here. For those of you who still don't understand, it is saying that if you are in Christ, you have nothing in common with unbelievers. God's Word said it, not me! Once you have made the confession of faith and accepted Jesus Christ as your Lord and

Savior, your life is hidden in Christ. You shouldn't be hanging out with the same people you once did. Why? Because you are now supposed to be walking in the light, just as Jesus Christ walked in the light. God has called us out of darkness into His marvelous light and that light is Jesus Christ. 2 Corin. 5:17 (NKJV) says, "Therefore, if anyone is in Christ, he is a new creation; old things have passed away; behold, all things have become new."

Now, in order to be a new creation in Christ, you have to die to self (the flesh). If there is no spiritual renewal of the mind, it will be hard to become a new creation. In other words, if you are still hanging out with the same old crowd doing the same old things before you confessed Christ, then there has not been a spiritual transformation. Therefore, you are not a new creation; you are still the same person you were before you confessed Christ. I know you may be saying, "What's wrong with hanging out with my old friends?" Well, here is what 1 Corin.15:33-34 (NKJV) has to say about it: "Do not be deceived: Evil company corrupts good habits. Awake to righteousness, and do not sin; for some do not have the knowledge of God. I speak this to your shame." "What does that mean?" you may be asking yourself. Nine times out of ten, if you keep hanging around the same people you use to sin with, chances are you will find yourself doing the same things you used to do. No one hangs out with someone they do not have anything in common with.

When I was a little girl my mother used to always say, "Birds of a feather flock together." I had no idea what she meant by that, but now I understand. Whatever it is that you do, you will hookup with people who have the same mindset as you. Think about your life for a moment. What do you like to do? What type of people do you associate yourself with? What do you all have in common? You see my point?

"So He called them to Himself and said to them in parables: "How can Satan cast out Satan? If a kingdom is divided against itself, that kingdom cannot stand. And if a house is divided against itself, that house cannot stand. And if Satan has risen up against himself, and is divided, he cannot stand, but has an end. No one can enter a strong man's house and plunder his goods, unless he first binds the strong man. And then he will plunder his house" (NKJV, Mark 3:23-27).

See, the reason why people don't have a problem with being around others who have the same sin as they do is because they have the same sinful spirit dwelling inside of them. I know you may be saying, "How can I say something like that?" Well, "All unrighteousness is sin, and there is sin not leading to death" (NKJV, 1John 5:17).

Now don't get me wrong, there is nothing wrong with being around sinners. After all, we are in this world, but not of this world, and we will come in contact with the world on a daily basis. Even Jesus hung out among the sinners; but, the difference is Jesus associated Himself with sinners for one main goal, and that was to minister to them. He didn't hang out with them just for the sake of hanging out with them. Nor did He partake in the sinful behavior they did. Do you see the difference? Once Jesus Christ ministered to them, their lives changed and they followed Him. How many lives have changed because you've ministered to someone who does not know Christ? Or, are you just hanging out with sinners just for the sake of it and participating in the same sinful behavior as they are? Examine yourself to see whether your motive for hanging out with sinners is to minister to them or to partake in the same sins. After all, what communion does light have with darkness? Do not be deceived!

"It is the spirit who gives life; the flesh profits nothing. The words that I speak to you are spirit, and they are life. But there are some of you who do not believe" (NKJV, John 6:63&64). Will you mess up? Sure, you will, because of your disobedience to the word of God; however, the more you study and meditate on the word of God, you will begin to transform from that old person you used to be. Listen to what God tells us! "But you are a chosen generation, a royal priesthood, a holy nation, His own special people, that you may proclaim the praises of Him who called you out of darkness into His marvelous light; who once were not a people but are now the people of God, who had not obtained mercy but now have obtained mercy"(NKJV, 1Peter 2:9&10). You should be thanking God right now for the blood of Jesus Christ who justified (made you right with God) you by dying on the cross for your sins. So, if you've messed up, repent of your sins and God will forgive you of your sins. God is all-knowing! God knows we are going to mess up, but He wants us to come to Him when we do.

"Flee also youthful lusts; but pursue righteousness, faith, love, peace with those who call on the Lord out of a pure heart. In humility correcting those who are in

opposition, if God perhaps will grant them repentance, so that they may know the truth, and that they may come to their senses and escape the snare of the devil, having been taken captive by him to do his will" (NKJV, 2Tim.2:22, 25-26).

Jesus Christ died so that we could go to the Father in prayer for ourselves. So, when you mess up (because you will-just keep living) do not tell your friends; those same friends you told your sins to will judge you. For those of you who don't think or won't admit that you sometimes will mess up read 1John 1:4-10.

Listen, it does not matter how good of a Christian you are or claim to be. If you are not rooted and grounded in God's word, you will find yourself doing exactly what the world does. For what fellowship hath righteousness (believers) with unrighteousness (nonbelievers)? And what communion hath light (believers) with darkness (nonbelievers)? If we call ourselves believers, we should be walking in righteousness - for Jesus Christ Himself is righteous. For those of you who are nonbelievers, you walk in darkness. Now, let me talk to the church folks - for those who only go to church out of habit (tradition), but don't have a relationship with Jesus

Christ.... the ones that sit in church Sunday after Sunday dressed all pretty, the ones who know of God's word, but choose to do things their own way. Here's the thing, if you are not applying and obeying God's word to your life, then it doesn't profit you anything because you are walking in darkness too. I understand that may seem harsh, but it is so true.

"And have no fellowship with the unfruitful works of darkness, but rather expose [rebuke] them" (NKJV, Eph. 5:11). Read verses 1-17 to get a clear understanding.

In order to have fellowship with someone, there has to be some type of relationship with that person. The key word in the scripture above is "unfruitful works." If the person you are hanging around is not about building the kingdom of God, you shouldn't want to hang out with them anyway. After all, you are a believer, right? There are only two people who know if you are truly a believer - you and God. What I am saying, in a nutshell, is this: you can't continue to hang out with those who walk in darkness and think their ways won't eventually rub off on you. Those are not really your friends anyway. What will end up happening is, as soon as you mess up they are going to talk about you. What is the first thing you think will come out their mouths? "And you call yourself a Christian!" Let me tell you just how good of a friend they are! They won't say it to you, but they will tell everybody else what you have done. Don't worry, though, because you will hear about it from someone else. So, when you hear about it don't get mad because you shouldn't have told them what you had done in the first place.

One thing you should remember is, Satan does not want to see the children of God obey the word of God. Why? Because Satan knows when Christ returns, God's people will reign in eternity (heaven) with God. God has already loosed Satan (read 1Peter 5:8) and he is going to try to take as many Christians to hell with him (if it were possible). Satan is not worried about nonbelievers, because he knows where they are going. Satan does not have any power, and we need to stop blaming him for everything. You know the old saying, "The devil made me do it," right? Well, that's the biggest lie ever told. We all have a choice whether to do right or wrong and good or evil. We are the ones who get ourselves into situations we shouldn't be in because of our selfish desires. Trust me, I have been there many times before. So, stop blaming Satan because he is powerless! Take responsibility for your own actions! No one can make you do anything (without putting a gun to your head), that you don't want to do. You knew it was wrong before you did it, but you did it anyway.

Listen to what Paul says in Rom.7:14-20(NKJV): *"For we know that the law is spiritual, but I am carnal, sold under sin. For what I am doing, I do not understand. For what I will to do, that I do not practice; but what I hate, that I do. If, then, I do what I will not to do, I agree with the law that it is good. But now, it is no longer I who do it, but sin that dwells in me. For I know that in me (that is, in my flesh) nothing good dwells; for to will is present with me, but how to perform what is good I do not find. For the good that I will to do, I do not do, but the evil I will not to do, that I practice. Now if I do what I will not to do, it is no longer I who do it, but sin that dwells in me." Read verses 21-24.* Do you understand what Paul is saying in this scripture? I don't care how good you think you are or how often you go or do not go to church. You are going to mess up! God knows exactly when, where, how, how often, the time, date, hour, minute, and second we are going to mess up. That is why Jesus died for our sins, so that we would be reconciled back to the Father. When God created Adam and Eve they were perfect (meaning complete and without sin), but when they sinned (disobeyed God's instructions), that brought about a separation between God and mankind. Let me throw this out there for free, because people are quick to blame God for their sinful acts or behavior. Mankind, that is the whole human race, is a byproduct of Adam and Eve. So, what I'm saying is, when they sinned, everyone after them has that same sinful nature dwelling on the inside of them. God's desire is for His creation to be reconciled to Him, because it pleases Him. Now remember, anyone after Adam and Eve is not a creation of God, but a byproduct of sin. I know that may be hard for some to digest, but it is the truth. For those who believe God created you to be intimate with people of the same sex, sin created you that way. Don't blame God for your lustful desires.

We need to totally depend on God in every area of our lives. What are you afraid of? What do you have to lose? Besides, you've tried everything else and it hasn't worked yet. I know it's going to be hard to stop trying to do things your way (God is still working on me too), but submit to the will of God. He is faithful to do what He has promised He will do. However, in order for

you to know what He has promised to do, you
have to spend time in His word. God's word
is truth and no lie. I dare you to start
spending time reading God's word. Then,
look at the things that are happening in the
world. You will quickly see how trustworthy
the word of God is because you will see God's
word fulfilling itself. God is not like man
that He should lie. God can be trusted!
Aren't you glad about that? I know I am,
because I've been lied to numerous times by
people throughout my life. When you've
been hurt by people who claim to love and
care for you, it makes it hard for you to put
your trust in anyone.

*"Do not trust in a friend; Do not put your
confidence in a companion; Guard the doors of your
mouth From her who lies in your bosom" (NKJV,
Micah 7:5).*

When we put our trust and confidence into
relationships, we set ourselves up to be hurt, lied too
or disappointed at some point or another in that
relationship. I'm not saying you shouldn't get into a
relationship with someone, but what I am saying is
to trust God to protect you in that relationship.

God is trustworthy, faithful, committed, and
loving. He will not do anything that would destroy
that relationship between you and Him. I dare you
to try Him for yourself. In trying Him, you must get

in His word to see what He has promised you. Once you know what His word says, believe it and apply it to your life. Trust ☺, you will not regret it!

Chapter 4

"Love Never Fails"

"Does not behave rudely, does not seek its own, is not provoked, thinks no evil; does not rejoice in iniquity, but rejoices in the truth;" (NKJV, 1 Corin. 13:5&6)

When it comes to relationships, the word "love" has been perverted. Society today has taken love out of its original context. Love is not just uttering words just for the sake of saying them. Love requires action. Love should not be used for sexual gain. 1 Corin. 13:4 (NKJV) states, "Love suffers long, and is kind; love does not envy, love does not parade itself, is not puffed up [arrogant]." Read all of chapter 13. Do you hear what is being said here? So, why is it that we find ourselves in relationships with people who do the opposite of these verses? Then again, we ourselves may be the one who does the opposite of these verses. A common cliché says love is blind, but it doesn't mean you have to put up with foolishness. If you find yourself crying rather than laughing, sad rather than happy, or stressed rather than blessed just maybe it's because you are looking for fulfillment in the wrong relationships. Instead of focusing on our relationship with God, we put all our focus and trust in relationships with men, women, material things, careers, etc.

"It is better to trust in the Lord Than to put confidence [trust] in man" (NKJV, Psalm 118:8).

For years and years, we have gotten that scripture wrong. We put our trust in everything except God. I will be the first to admit that I have been guilty of not putting my trust fully in God. At that time, I didn't have a relationship with God so I didn't know I was supposed to trust Him; but, I thank God that He opened my eyes to His word, and now I see how important it is to trust in Him and Him alone.

You know what amazes me? How we only run to God when relationships with men and women go bad, but then as soon as we get into another relationship with someone else, we forget all about God – not to mention, the only "relationship" we have with God is when things are going bad in our lives. Then, we want Him to help us. Again, as soon as things start looking good for us, we forget all about God. Yes, I am guilty too. How dare us! We have some nerves!

Throughout the Old Testament the children of Israel would only serve God when their backs were against the wall, and as soon as God delivered them out of the situation they were in, they turned their backs on Him. They would go back to worshipping their idols and doing other things that didn't bring glory to God. As soon as trouble came their way again, they would run back to God for Him to deliver them again. When we read those stories in the Old Testament we think, "How could they do that?" Actually, if we were honest with ourselves, we do the same thing to God today. Whatever we put before God (make our main focus) is an idol and that is what or who we worship. Whether it's our spouse, house, car, children, job, music, television, money, parents, or activities, it is an idol. We are too busy replacing God with people and things, which is a big no-no.

"Do not lay up for yourselves treasures on earth, where moth and rust destroy and where thieves break in and steal; but lay up for yourselves treasures in heaven, where

neither moth nor rust destroys and where thieves do not break in and steal. For where your treasure is, there your heart will be also" (NKJV, Matt.6:19-21).

Don't get me wrong, there is nothing wrong with having all these things, but when you put them before God, that's when there's a problem. "You shall not go after other gods, the gods of other peoples who are all around you. (for the Lord your God is a jealous God among you), lest the anger of the Lord your God be aroused against you and destroy you from the face of the earth" (NKJV, Deut. 6:14&15). Man! Don't we have this thing backwards! In essence, we treat God like a spare tire (the little donut tire), the one that stays in the trunk until we have a flat. Then, as soon as we get a new tire we put the spare tire right back in the trunk.

We should be thanking God for His grace and mercy. Because in the Old Testament, God would have destroyed the children of Israel for worshipping idol gods. God commands us not to place anything before Him. When we replace God with the things of this world, we are being disobedient to God. God is so good, though! He loves us so much that He gives us chance after chance to get it right with Him.

"For you, brethren, have been called to liberty [freedom]; only do not use liberty as an opportunity for the flesh, but through love serve one another" (NKJV, Galatians 5:13).

Man, I am so thankful, because I have messed that up over and over again! Yeah, you will mess up too, but we should learn from our mistakes or from the mistakes of others. Like the old saying goes, "When you know better, you should do better." You should not continue to do the same things over and over again, especially if you are a child of God. Because as soon as things are not going well in your life (or the way you think it should go), you wonder why or you blame God for your mess; but, if you would stop doing the same old mess, then maybe you will have more mountain top experiences rather than valley low disappointments. Trust me, I know, because I have learned the hard way! Don't get me wrong, though, because those valley low disappointments will and are going to come, but they are designed to make you a stronger and better person fit for the kingdom of heaven. However, if you are rooted and grounded in God's word, you will handle the situation(s) differently than you would if you were in the world. See, you can stand on God's promise that says, "God is our refuge and strength, A very present help in trouble" (NKJV, Psalms 46:1).

God loves us so much that He wants us to cast all cares upon Him, for He cares for us (NKJV, 1Peter 5:7, paraphrased). Now *that's* love! You know where the problem comes in? When we don't cast ALL of our cares on God. If God was not able to handle all our cares, He wouldn't have told us to do so. That's just one of the promises of God. If you don't know what His word says, then you will never trust Him to handle your cares. We try to handle the situation ourselves and then wonder why God is not moving in our lives. STOP! God does not need our help. He didn't need us when He created the heavens and earth or when He gave the sea its decree. So do you think He needs our help when it comes to fixing our mess? God knows all about our situations. As a matter of fact, He knows about everything that goes on in our lives. There is nothing that we can hide from God, and in order for us to get help from God, we must cry out to Him for the help that we need and stop going to everyone and everything else. I know that's going to be hard to do, because it was really hard for me. When I was going through a difficult situation in my life, my friend use to say, "Olympia let it go. Give that thing over to God. If you don't you will run yourself crazy." It took me some time, I do admit, but I let it go. So, what am I saying? Whatever the problem is let it go and let God work it out for your good. Even though we are not worthy, God loves us enough that He will deliver us from the mess that we created. Isn't God good and worthy of all praise, honor, and glory?

The love of God will never fail. His love is not temporal, shady, unseemly, conniving, conditional or based on falsehood. The love of God will last for eternity, is based on truth, is not hidden, is pure, and is unconditional.

Chapter 5

"Step Up to the Plate"

"Nevertheless, because of sexual immorality, let each man have his own wife, and let each woman have her own husband" *(NKJV, 1 Corin.7:2).*

To get a clear understanding of the above scripture you would have to go back and read 1 Corin.6:13-20. Yet, verse 2 is very clear. So why is it that we have so much sexual immorality in the church?

"Flee sexual immorality. Every sin that a man does is outside the body, but he who commits sexual immorality sins against his own body" *(NKJV, 1 Corin.6:18).*

The church has gotten away from teaching about sexual immorality. Yet, sexual immorality is running rampant in the church. Something is wrong with that picture! It's funny how the world, television, music, videos, and friends are teaching our children that it's okay to have sex as long as they are protecting themselves, but no one is telling them that it is wrong to have sex outside of marriage. No one is telling them that premarital sex, adultery, and fornication are sin.

When I was growing up, no one told me how important it was to save myself for marriage. No one told me that premarital sex is a sin against God. Sex was not a subject that was talked about where I'm from – as far as being right or wrong. We (my cousins, brother and myself) would be in the next room when our parents were watching sexually explicit moves on television. So, you know what we were doing as kids, right? We would sneak outside the door and watch without them seeing us. Or, we would find the dirty magazines that they hid and look at the nasty pictures. Parents, it's time we talk to our children and tell them why they should wait to have sex. Don't just tell them that it is okay as long as they protect themselves. God will and is going to hold you accountable for not teaching your child/children what is right in His eyes. Now, if they go out there and have sex (whether protected or unprotected) after you have told them what God has to say about premarital sex, you will not be held accountable. Tell them, they should not only wait because of pregnancy and diseases, but let them know what matters the most. Let them know that above pregnancy and diseases, it is a sin against God.

Oh, and the subject about sex is not just for teenagers, but it's for adults too. All too often, we try to put sin on a scale between one to ten ("One" being not so bad and "ten" being the worst). When it comes to sin, there is not a difference. One who commits murder and one who commits sexual immorality have this in common - sin. No sin is greater than the other; it's all the same. God does not view sin according to a scale. To God, sin is sin! All forms of sexual immorality are sins against God. God intended sex to be enjoyed between a husband and his wife. Notice, I said a husband and his wife, not someone else's husband or wife. And He certainly didn't intend for sex to be used for the purpose of same sex relationships or marriage. Sexual immorality is unfaithfulness, rejection, and idolatry towards God, and unless you repent, sexual immorality will lead to death.

"For the wages of sin is death, but the gift of God is eternal life in Christ Jesus our Lord" (NKJV, Romans 6:23).

Now, don't get me wrong, because you will still have to give an account to God for your actions. I do not think anyone really realizes the seriousness of sexual immorality (I know I didn't at some point in my life). Or is it that we really don't care what God thinks? Sexual immorality defiles the temple of God (which is your body), separates the relationship between God and mankind, destroys marriages, and breaks the covenant between husbands and wives.

"Or do you not know that your body is the temple of the Holy Spirit who is in you, whom you have from God, and you are not your own" (NKJV, 1Corin.6:19)?

Boy, we sure have gotten that scripture wrong for years and years! See, we think our bodies belong to us and we can do whatever we want when we want. But, our bodies do not belong to us, they belong to God! "For you were bought at a price; [which is the shedding of Jesus' blood] therefore glorify God in your body and in your spirit, which are God's" (NKJV, 1Corin.6:20). That scripture was an eye opener for me. It is clear and straight to the point! There should not be any misunderstandings about it. Unless, of course, you just want to be blatantly disobedient to the word of God.

As believers, it's time we take our walk with Jesus Christ seriously. People often say I'm too holy, and there was a time when I would have had a problem with people saying that about me; nonetheless, when I came into the knowledge that God requires us to be holy, it didn't bother me anymore. So, it's time for us to stop playing church. Either we are going to be obedient or disobedient to God - there are no gray areas. We are either for God or against Him. I admit, I haven't always done things right, but when you know better you should do better. When Jesus died, He died that we would be delivered from our sins. The problem is, we keep falling into the same old holes over and over again. Jesus died so that we would be set free from the bondage of sin and death. He died that we would have a right to the tree of life. What does that mean? We no longer have to live a life of sin. Sin only brings about guilt and shame. So, don't worry if someone know the things you used to do or who you once were, because Jesus has cleansed you with His blood. Not only that, but if you have confessed your sins to God, He has forgiven you. Say it with me, "Thank you Lord!" I used to worry about what others thought and knew about me, but I don't have that worry anymore. Jesus says in (NKJV, John 8:7b), "He who is without sin among you, let him throw a stone at her first." In other words, how can you point out what someone else has done? What about you? What have you done? Better yet, what are you doing now? Your life isn't squeaky clean! How can you talk about someone else when you are doing wrong yourself? Check yourself! There used to be a song that went something like this, "Sweep around your own front door before you try to sweep around mine." I know some of you know how that song goes. Get your life right first, before you try to talk about someone else. And, if you are judging (forming an opinion) about someone based on who they used to be or for what they used to do, then you are wrong. That is a sin too! It is called gossiping!

Step up to the plate! 1Thess. 4:3 (NKJV) says, "For this is the will of God, your [make it personal] sanctification: that you should abstain from sexual immorality." Read verses 4-7 to get a clear understanding of verse 3. Paul was speaking to those who know or claim to know God. Yes, that's right, Paul was speaking to believers. When Jesus died on the cross He sanctified us by His blood. What does that mean? That means, as believers, we are set apart from the world. We should not be doing the same thing the world does. There should be a difference between believers (the body of Christ) and nonbelievers (the world). Instead, there is no difference between believers and the world. The church today is no different from the world. We are copying the habits of the world, rather than the world copying us as believers. Why is that? Because we are not living according to the word of God so the world doesn't know what to believe. We say one thing, but the way we live our lives tell another story. How can we lead the world to Christ if they can't see Christ in us? The world is watching us! They don't want to hear a sermon; they want to see how we live our lives as Christians. After all, people who we come in contact with everyday (coworkers, friends, associates, and family members) know we go to church. They want to see if we are going to mess up so they can say, "See, that's why I don't go to church because there are a bunch of hypocrites at that church." How can we be a witness of the gospel if we are living unseemly?

"Abstain from every form of evil. Now may the God of peace Himself sanctify you completely; and may your whole spirit, soul, and body be preserved blameless at the

coming of our Lord Jesus Christ" (NKJV, *1Thess.5:22-23).*

If we do not abstain ourselves from every form of evil, how then are we set apart from the world? We are not nor can we be! If we continue to associate ourselves with every form of evil, then we are just like the world.

In the book of James, James tells us, "Let no one say when he is tempted, I am tempted by God; for God cannot be tempted by evil, nor does He Himself tempt anyone. But each one is tempted when he is drawn away by his own desires and enticed" (NKJV, James 1:13-14). What is James saying? No one made you do whatever it was you did. You did it because that's what you wanted to do. What's in you will eventually come out. After all, remember we were born into this world with a sinful nature. **Side bar, side bar! Warning! Those desires could be gossip, adultery, fornication, homosexuality, filthiness, covetousness, lying, stealing, filthy communication, coarse gesturing, disobedience, pride, idolatry, greed, and selfishness (the list goes on). Any form of evil! You get the picture? With every sin there are consequences. Sin separates us from God! And where there is sin, there can be no fellowship with God, unless you truly repent and turn away from your sins. Turning away means not repeating the same sin again and again and again. Oh, just so you know, you will still have to pay for the sins you have committed even after you ask for forgiveness.

"Then, when desire has conceived, it gives birth to sin; and sin, when it is full-grown, brings forth death" (NKJV, James 1:15).

Wow! If we really understood that sin brings forth death, we would think twice about doing those things that God commands us not to do. We say we love God on one hand, and on the other hand our actions show different. What that says to me is that we don't care about what God commands us to do. That's just like someone saying they love someone, but every time you turn around they are mistreating or hurting that person. It would be hard to believe that person loves them, right? Well, think about it: we do the same thing to God. We say we love Him with our mouth, but our actions show different. Children of God, it's time for us to step up to the plate and walk (apply God's word to our lives) according to the word of God. God is not concerned about our words. He looks at our heart. He wants us to live a life that is holy and pleasing unto Him. Words are not enough! We have to live according to the scripture. As believers, God has a higher standard for us. And that standard is according to His word and His word alone.

"but as He who called you is holy, you also be holy in all your conduct, because it is written, "Be holy, for I am holy" (NKJV, 1Peter 1:15-16). Read all Chapter 1.

God has called us out of darkness! So why do we continue to do the same foolish things time and time again? Could it be that we are in darkness? Read Ephesians 5:8-11. Do you not care about the pain and agony Christ had to endure for your sins? Come on! Don't you want to live a better life? Being a Christian is more than just going to church Sunday after Sunday. We treat church as if we are punching a time clock. We come to church, listen to the Preacher, sing in or direct the choir, usher, serve in hospitality, sit in the pulpit, and serve as a deacon, but as soon as church is over we go back to living lives that are not pleasing to God. I was guilty of that at one point in my life too. I thank God for showing me how I'm supposed to live as a Christian. 2Peter 2:21-22 (NKJV) says, "For it would have been better for them not to have known the way of righteousness, than having known it, to turn from the holy commandment delivered to them. But it has happened to them according to the true proverb: "A dog returns to his own vomit," and, "a sow, having washed, to her wallowing in the mire." That is why it is so important to stay rooted and grounded in the word of God. It is so easy to slip back into the old things we use to do.

As believers, we need to make God/Jesus Christ our main focus. If not, we will find ourselves in the same whirlwind of sin we've been in all our lives. Aren't you tired of being held down in chains from the lustful desires of your flesh? Oh, if only you would realize that you have been set free from the bondage of sin by the blood of Jesus Christ.

In Lacrae's song "Live Free" (ft. Sho Baraka and Jai), Jai says,

> I'm free from sin I win, I win
>
> I'm free, I'm free
>
> And no more chains are holdin' me
>
> I'm free from death
>
> Got power now, me kill the flesh
>
> I'm free, I'm free

I'm gone, I'm gone.

If Jesus Christ has set you free from sin, why are you still a prisoner in your own house (that is your body)? My mom always taught me, when someone does something for you, always say "Thank you," because they didn't have to do it. So say it with me, "Thank You Jesus Christ for dying in my place out on the cross at Calvary for the sins I have committed." Now, repent of those sins and ask God for forgiveness.

Chapter 6

"Commitment"

"If a man makes a vow to the Lord, or swears an oath to bind himself by some agreement he shall not break his word; he shall do according to all that proceeds out of his mouth" (NKJV, Numbers 30:2).

When it comes to relationships, no one takes the word commitment seriously. There used to be a time when people would say, "A man's word is his bond." Sounds good, right? But how much value does that hold today? It's really amazing to see so many people who say they are Christians commit to everything else but God. They commit to their jobs, hobbies, television, video games, their spouse, their children, school, sporting events, shopping, cars, and the list goes on. Yet, if you were to ask them where does God fit on their list of commitments, He would probably be at the bottom of that list. I know you are probably say, "How can she say something like that?" Well, just check your list of commitments and see where God is on that list. If everything on your list of commitments take priority over God, then how can you say you are committed to Him? Meditate on this for a moment! Whatever or whomever you spend time with the most (put first in your life) shows what or who you are committed too. As shameful as it is, I used to be there too! But God's word opened my eyes to what is important to Him.

"Commit your works to the Lord, And your thoughts will be established" (NKJV, Proverbs 16:3). Read verses 1&2.

Overall, I'm not saying you can't have fun. As Christians, we can have fun without compromising who we are in Christ; however, if you find yourself doing everything else except spending time with God (praying, reading the word of God, serving God, attending church and fellowshipping with other believers), you may want to check your commitment to God.

"All the ways of a man are pure in his own eyes, But the Lord weighs the spirits" (NKJV, Prov.16:2). You can't fool God!

Let me tell you a little secret: whatever or whoever you are committed to also shows where your heart is. God knows your heart! You may put on a front on Sundays, but God knows who you truly are. We need to be serious about our commitment we've made to God. Where there is no commitment, there is no relationship. It is impossible to have a relationship with someone without being committed to them or spending time with them. Therefore, how can we say we have a relationship with God if we are not committed to Him or never spend time with Him?

Matt. 6:24 (NKJV) says, "No one can serve two masters; for either he will hate the one and love the other, or else he will be loyal to the one and despise the other. You cannot serve God and mammon." I know you are saying, "I go to church every Sunday." Well, only you and God know if you are truly committed to Him or not. After all, God does not look at outward appearance like man; He looks at the heart. See, here is where we get caught up! We look at the outward appearance of a person not knowing what truly lies in their heart. And then, when their heart reveals the true person, we are shocked and can't believe it. A person can clean up really good when you first meet them, but pressure burst pipes. Whatever lies in the heart of a person will eventually come out. "The heart is deceitful above all things, And desperately wicked; Who can know it? I, the Lord, search the heart, I test the mind, Even to give every man according to his ways, According to the fruit of his doings" (Jer. 17:9&10 NKJV). God does not care about what you look like on the outside; He searches the heart! So, you may think you are getting over on someone else, but God knows your heart. Therefore, if there is deceit in your heart, how can you be committed to someone? If you think about lying, stealing, murder, adultery, fornication, gossip, etc., that's who you are. There's nothing wrong with thinking about something, right? Wrong. Scripture says, "A good man out of the good treasure of his heart brings forth good; and an evil man out of the evil treasure of his heart brings forth evil; For out of the abundance of the heart his mouth speaks" (NKJV, Luke 6:45). As believers, we should not take pleasure in things that does not bring glory to God. Period!

People think just because they come to church Sunday after Sunday, is the president of an auxiliary, a deacon, sings in the choir, ushers on the usher board, is a preacher/pastor or minister, is a member, or whatever their title is, that they can live a life not pleasing to God. And the tragedy is, they think God is pleased just because they hold a certain position in the church.

For years, we've believed the devil is red, has two horns, a pitch fork, and a long tail. Well, Satan sits in the church every Sunday, and sometimes he's the first one there. If we would take a look in the mirror and be honest with ourselves, we would see exactly what Satan looks like. Our actions reveal who we truly are! How we live, treat others and react to things speaks volumes to who we serve.

"But if your eye is bad, your whole body will be full of darkness. If therefore the light that is in you is darkness, how great is that darkness!" (NKJV, Matt.6:23)

You may not murder, steal, or commit adultery, but if you gossip, fornicate, envy, have bitterness toward a person, cannot forgive, are jealous, have hate in your heart, think evil, are a busybody, are lazy, disobedient, and you talk about people, are you not guilty of sin? Sin is sin no matter how great or small. Sin does not and cannot bring glory to God! So, just because you come to church and "serve" in some type of way, God does not accept what you are doing because of your sin(s). Remember the story of Cain and Abel. See Genesis 4.

You cannot be a part of the kingdom of heaven if you live a life of sin. "Many will say to Me in that day, 'Lord, Lord, have we not prophesied in Your name, cast out demons in Your name, and done many wonders in Your name?' And then I [Jesus Christ] will declare to them, 'I never knew you; depart from Me, you who practice lawlessness" (NKJV, Matt.7:22&23)! Jesus Christ was not talking to the heathens; He was speaking to those who claim to be Christians. WOW! If we are going to be Christians (Christ like), then we need to take our walk with Christ serious. After all, we made a commitment to follow and obey the commandments God has left for us. Again I say, it's timeout for playing church!

Chapter 7

"Submission"

"Wives, submit to your own husbands, as to the Lord" (NKJV, Eph. 5:22).

This chapter is going to be a touchy subject for many people to receive. Ladies, please don't let the title or scripture reference throw you off. This chapter is for both men and women.

I know what we have been taught by other women when it comes to submitting to our husband. Or we have heard them say, "I'm not being submissive to him. I'm a grown woman. He can't tell me what to do." But you know what happens when you listen and act on bad advice, right? Bad things end up happening. That is why some of those women that gave you bad advice about being submissive to your husband are either divorced, single or having problems within their marriage.

Unless your husband is asking you to sin, you are to be submissive to him in all things. Yes, that is right, in ALL things. I know what you may be asking yourself, "What if he is not saved?" Even if he is not saved, you are still required to be submissive to him unless he is asking you to sin.

"Therefore, just as the church is subject to Christ, so let the wives be to their own husbands in everything" (NKJV, Ephesians 5:24).

Now, those are not my words - but God's. Read Ephesians 5 in its entirety. It will open up your understanding from the bad advice we have gotten about being submissive. One of the main reasons a lot of people have a problem with submission is because they have not submitted themselves to the Lord. Ladies, just a little side note, there is nothing wrong with submitting to your own husband. Is God greater than your husband? Ultimately, we are not submitting to our husbands; we are submitting unto God. And in submitting to God we are being submissive to our own husband.

I want to talk to the ladies, my sisters in Christ who are married. The reason why some of your husbands don't attend church with you is because you don't act like a woman of God. Now, I understand that may not be the case in every woman's life, but the percentages are high. If he was not going to church with you or on his own before you all were married, what made you think he was going to change? I'm not saying every man is like that, but women are the majority in the church, so you do the math.

Women of God, if you and your husband attend church and serve in some capacity together regularly, say "Thank you Lord." When I say women of God, I'm talking to those of you who have accepted Christ as Savior and fully understand why He is called Savior. I'm speaking to women who are truly following after Jesus Christ. I'm talking to women who are walking in obedience to the word of God. I'm not talking to those who were baptized as a child because you were forced to get baptized, yet your life does not reflect the life of Jesus Christ. Also, just because you *know of* Jesus does not mean you have a relationship with Him. I know, I know, you were raised in the church all your life, right? But, did you have a personal relationship with Jesus Christ for yourself when you were growing up? In other words, were you walking in obedience to the word of God as a child? See, people think just because their mother made them go to church when they were a child, that it means they have a relationship with Jesus Christ. Well, I hate to be the bad news bandit! Just because you were raised in the church "all your life," doesn't mean you are saved or have a relationship with Jesus Christ. People think just because they were baptized as a child that they have a relationship with Jesus Christ as an adult. This is not the case. How you live your life determines the type of relationship you have with God. Baptism does not save you! Ask me how I know! Well, I was baptized at an early age because I saw my cousin getting baptized. It looked fun to me so I wanted to go down in the water just like she did. I did not understand anything about baptism nor did I confess Jesus Christ as my Lord and Savior. After I was baptized, I don't think I went back to that church again. And it's crazy because when I graduated from High School, the church where I was baptized sent me a Bible with my name engraved on the front.

Baptism is an outward expression of an inward conversion that you have died to your old sinful nature and have been risen with Christ in the newness of life that is in Christ Jesus. What you are saying is that you will obey all (not some) the commands that Christ Jesus has set. Jesus Christ was about His Father's business. He was obedient to the point of death. Confessing and believing that Jesus Christ is Savior and Lord will save you. It goes deeper than that; again, you have to obey every word of God and apply God's word to your life. And here is the most important thing, you must go share the gospel of Jesus Christ with those who don't know Him. You have to tell others how Jesus Christ died for your sin. You must share the gospel with sinners. Also, you have to have faith in God. Faith without works is dead!

"But without faith it is impossible to please Him, for he who comes to God must believe that He is, and that He is a rewarder of those who diligently seek Him" (NKJV, Hebrews 11:6).

Sisters in Christ, how can your husband see Christ in you if you raise more "H-E double hockey sticks" than he does? 1Peter 3:1&2 (NKJV) says, "Wives, likewise, be submissive to your own husbands, that even if some do not obey the word, they, without a word, may be won by the conduct of their wives, when they observe your chaste conduct accompanied by fear." Now the scripture says, "even if some do not obey the word," right? I'm going to let you in on a little secret; just because people go to church doesn't mean they always obey the word of God. Oh, don't get me wrong, they clean up really good on the outside to make you think they are obedient to God. They step in church with their nice suits, dresses, ties, shoes, hats, smelling good, hair done/cut, and are well-manicured; they are even driving nice big cars, but their lives don't reflect Christ. Ultimately, God knows the heart and thoughts of every man, woman, boy, and girl.

This section is for both men and women. Even though someone is not acting like or is not a Christian, we as believers must always conduct ourselves as followers of Christ. That means you have to take a self-examination of yourself daily to see if you are walking in obedience to the word of God. When you self-examine yourself, the word of God should always be your guide, not man. "But be doers of the word, and not hears only, deceiving yourselves. For if anyone is a hearer of the word and not a doer, he is like a man observing his natural face in a mirror; for he observes himself, goes away, and immediately forgets what kind of man he was" (NKJV, James 1:22-24). You can't just listen to or read the word of God; you have to apply the Word to your life daily.

God cannot be fooled! He knows if you are only a hearer and not a doer of His word. And you know what, so do you. Just look at your life! How are you living? What are you doing or not doing? Be honest with yourself, because God knows all about you. He knows you better than you know yourself. You know what amazes me, how people think they don't have to obey those who have authority (the man of God) over them, but they can obey God. If you can't obey the man of God who God appointed over you, how can you obey God? Can you separate the two?

"Remember those who rule over you, who have spoken the word of God to you, whose faith follow, considering the outcome of their conduct" (NKJV, Hebrews 13:7).

According to the world, if you submit to someone it means that you are weak or soft, and that's where the problem comes in when it relates to the church. We still have the same mindset as the world; that's why we have a hard time submitting to God -

because we will not submit to the man of God that God has placed over us. Here's what we do not realize though: the man of God, your Pastor, is there to govern you with the word of God that you may obey it. So, in essence, it is God that you are submitting yourself to, because the man of God represents God. I know, I know, no one wants to be known as being weak or soft. That is why we still try to do things our way. And what really gets me is we think we can serve God without submitting ourselves totally to Him. Submit means to surrender or yield to the will or authority of another. When you submit to God you are saying, "Lord, I surrender my all to You." In other words, you are dying to the way you used to think, act, view things, and how you treat others. Being a Christian is not about us, but it's about Jesus Christ. Once we confessed Jesus Christ as our Lord and Savior, our life does not belong to us anymore. We belong to God!

"who once was not a people but are now the people of God, who had not obtained mercy but now have obtained mercy" (NKJV, 1Peter2:10).

Ladies, it's time we start acting like the women God is calling us to be. Always remember, no matter how hard we try, we cannot change our husband. Only God can change a person! He changed you, didn't He? If you are going to change, you must be willing to die to yourself and yield to God. So again, stop trying to change your husband and allow God to change him – it's not that you have to *let* God do anything anyway; He doesn't need your help. You are not your husband's savior! You did not die for his sins; Jesus Christ did.

Where are my single sisters in Christ? Continue to focus on God and do what He is calling you to do. Remain faithful to God and when He sees fit, He will bring you your Boaz (husband). We always look at being single as a bad thing, because of what we have been taught or seen. Trust me, I thought the same way at one point in my life.

When you are single, that should be the time that you develop a relationship with Jesus Christ, not focusing on how lonely you are or spending all your time looking for a man. Proverbs 18:22 (NKJV) says, "He who finds a wife finds a good thing, And obtains favor from the Lord." So, stop looking for a man, and put your focus on Jesus Christ, and that man who God has for you will find you. There is a blessing attached to a man finding a wife; he obtains favor from the Lord. God knows what you need and what you don't need. That is why He tried to shield you from some of those bad relationships you have been involved in, but you were so determined to have that man, so God allowed it to happen. Then, God showed you why He didn't want you to be in that relationship in the first place.

Even now, God knows that you are not ready for a relationship. That may be why He hasn't answered your prayer about sending you a husband. What will end up happening is, as soon as you get married, you will spend all your time trying to please your husband and will forget about God. You don't believe me? Just look at your past relationships. Before you started dating, you were going to church and serving God. As soon as Slick Ricky came along, you stop going to church or you weren't consistent anymore. Then, as time went by, God was no longer in the picture. Eventually, that relationship went bad and you ran back to God/church. Hold your head up! You are not alone. I was once there, and there are a lot of people that are there right now. And there is good news: You don't have to be there! Just focus on your relationship with Jesus Christ and be faithful to the things of God. In God's timing, He will bring you the man that He has for you.

"But I want you to be without care. He who is unmarried cares for the things of the Lord-how he may please the Lord. But he who is married cares about the things of the world-how he may please his wife. There is a difference between a wife and a virgin. The unmarried woman cares about the things of the Lord, that she may be holy both in body and in spirit. But she who is married cares about the things of the world-how she may please her husband" (NKJV, 1 Corinthians 7:32-34).

Why do you think you are not married? God knows once you are married, you will not be concerned about pleasing Him. You will only be concerned about pleasing your husband. So, whether you are a single man (looking for a wife) or single woman (waiting on your Boaz), use this time to get to know who Jesus Christ is. Find out who He says you are. Let Him lead and guide you into the man (husband) and woman (wife) of God He intends for you to be. Then, when you do get married, your marriage will bring praise, glory and honor to Him. I know you may get lonely, but replace that loneliness with a love for God and watch God move in your life. Being lonely does not mean you are alone; you are never alone when you have God. As Christians, we should be about our Father's business, not our own agendas, desires, thoughts, and actions. Everything we say and do should bring glory, honor, and praise to our Father.

Submit unto the Lord in everything you say and do. Don't worry about what others may say, think, or do to you. Keep your eyes on God! Remember, we are to suffer for Christ's sake. After all, He suffered for our sake when He was beaten and hung on the cross for our sins.

Chapter 8

"Covenant Relationship"

*"Nevertheless I have this against you,
that you have left your first love" (NKJV,
Rev.2:4).*

Often times throughout our life, we
long to be loved and accepted. Whether it's
from our parents, grandparents, spouse,
children, friends, siblings, girlfriends, or
boyfriends, we desire to be loved and
accepted. We make people and things our
main focus, and God is nowhere in the
picture. As soon as something bad happens,
we run to God. Then, when our life is back
on track (so to speak) we forget all about
God. We don't even realize that it was God
who brought us through that situation.

We value people and things more than
we value our relationship with God. God is

the creator of all things. He desires us to have a personal relationship with Him. "Remember now your Creator in the days of your youth, Before the difficult days come, And the years draw near when you say, I have no pleasure in them" (NKJV, Ecc. 12:1). Don't just call on God when life starts beating you down; praise Him in the good and bad times.

This brings me back to when my husband and I took our wedding vows. We entered into a covenant with God as well as with one another - to love one another for better or worse, for richer or poor, in sickness and health, forsaking all others, until death do us part. Well, that's the type of love we should have for and with God. I admit, I haven't always been in that type of love affair with God. It took me a long time to develop a love affair with God because of my lack of commitment to Him. Loving Him through the good and bad times; whether I had money or I was broke; when I was sick or healthy. And whether I was in a relationship with someone or not. See, what I didn't realize is I allowed people, material things, money, and sin be my god. What are you allowing to separate you from God?

"I make this covenant and this oath, not with you alone, but with him who stands

here with us today before the Lord our God, as well as with him who is not here with us today" (NKJV, Deuteronomy 29:14&15).

Marriage is based on a covenant relationship between God, a man, and a woman and it should not be easily broken. In the movie "Not Easily Broken" by T.D. Jakes, Dave Johnson (played by Morris Chestnut) and his wife, Clarice (played by Taraji P. Henson), seemed to have it all together on the outside, but they were struggling within their marriage. Clarice was in a terrible car accident that left her with a bad leg injury. In order for her to fully recover from the leg injury she had to go through physical therapy. Clarice allowed her selfishness and the bitterness of her mother to cloud her mind when it came to her husband. Then, tragedy struck! Over time, Dave found solace in the arms of Clarice's therapist because of his issues with his wife. Although, nothing major happened between Dave and the therapist, Dave realized the importance of his relationship with his wife. Clarice finally came to her senses and realized that her husband was more important than her selfishness, career and the bitterness of her mother.

Likewise, our relationship with God is based on a covenant relationship that should not be easily broken, because of our selfishness or whatever situation we may find ourselves in. I need you to really pay attention to what I'm about to say. God does not break His covenant or promises He made to us. The problem is we break our covenant and promises to Him because of a man, woman, money, jobs/careers, material things, just to name a few. The very thought of that just vexes my spirit when I look back at where I once was. Do you ever think about that? We expect God to keep His promises to us, but we can't keep our covenant with Him. We don't want to have anything to with God unless we want Him to do something for us. Who do we think we are? We got it all messed up. I use to be one of those people who would break my covenant and promises to God. The only time I had some kind of relationship with God was when I was stuck between a rock and a hard place. I would plead for God to get me out of whatever mess I got myself in. I would say, "Lord if you get me out of this situation I won't do it again." Boy, who was I kidding? As soon as God would bring me through a situation, I was right back in it again. I know some of you are probably downing your nose at me right now, but if you would be honest with yourself, you've done the same thing too.

Before I had a relationship with God, I admit, I didn't care about Him at all. Because if I would have cared about God, I would have respected Him in everything I said and did. The truth of the matter is, I didn't care about God or Jesus Christ because I didn't know or want to know them at the time. Even after I started to develop some type of relationship with God, I still messed up. But, I thank God that He loves me so much that He sent His One and Only Son to die for my sins that I might be redeemed back to Him. Not only that, once I repented of my sins, He forgave me and didn't kill me in my mess. Hallelujah! Thank you Jesus! If you don't have a relationship with someone, how can you respect them? If you are in a relationship with someone, your actions will show how much you respect, care, honor, and love them.

God has commanded us, "You shall love the Lord your God with all your heart, with all your soul, and with all your strength" (MKJV, Deut. 6:5). Here lies the problem when it comes to loving God: Our heart is far from Him. We are too busy loving (pleasing) ourselves, spouses, children, parents, material things, money, and careers, rather than loving God. Anything that you put before God is your god.

Remember what God said in our opening scripture? If you don't remember, go back to the beginning of this chapter and read the scripture under the title. God is a loving God, but He is also a jealous God and a God of wrath. Okay, hold up! I know you are probably saying, "How can God be loving and jealous and a God of wrath?" Well, don't you love your children and you still discipline them? Case closed! See, we think we can do or say whatever we want and there be no consequences. Well, sorry to break the bad news to you, but that's not how things work.

"I am the Lord your God who brought you out of the land of Egypt, out of the house of bondage [slavery]. You shall have no other gods before Me" (NKJV, Deut. 5:6&7).

Now, your bondage may be usury, disobedience, lying, cursing, stealing, pornography (which is a form of adultery), adultery, gossip, malice, backbiting, hatred, envy, greed, jealousy, sex, or covetousness. Those are just a few things that hinder us from loving and having a relationship with God. If you are in bondage to sin, there can be no fellowship with God. Why do you think we continue to sin? We continue to sin because our first nature is to sin and we do not fear (reverence) God. If we do not fear

God, how can we say we respect His word? When we continue to sin over and over again, we are saying, "I don't care what God's word says, I'm going to do things my way." What fellowship does light have with darkness? You do know that if you are walking in sin you are in darkness, right? I do not know what may be keeping you in bondage, but God can and will bring you out. All you have to do is repent and have faith that He will do it.

Here is the problem with being held in bondage! We are too busy loving the things of this world instead of God. FYI: If you place yourself before God, that's a sin too. God is not concerned about material things and all the things of this world. He desires a personal relationship with you. After all, we were originally created to worship God, but when sin entered into the world, things got messed up. Instead of worshipping God, we worship everything and everybody else.

"Do not love the world or the things in the world. If anyone loves the world, the love of the Father is not in him. For all that is in the world – the lust of the flesh, the lust of the eyes, and the pride of life – is not of the Father but is of the world. And the world is passing away, and the lust of it; but he

who <u>does the</u> <u>will</u> of God abides forever"
(NKJV, 1John 2:15-17 emphasis added).

Saints of God, just because we are in the world doesn't mean we are of this world. Let's start acting like the men and women of God we were called to be.

Chapter 9

"Why We Crave Love"

"You shall love the Lord your God with all your heart, with all your soul, and with all your strength. And these words which I command you today shall be in your heart" *(NKJV, Deuteronomy 6:5&6).*

Why do we crave love? I bet you thought I would never get to this, right? God commands us to love Him, because God is love. However, you cannot love the Lord your God with all your heart, soul and strength if He is not your God. What do I mean by that? Well, if you are not in a relationship with Jesus Christ, how then can you love Him? Most of us have a vicarious relationship with God based on what we have heard about Him, but we don't truly know Him for ourselves. As a matter of fact, every time He tries to introduce Himself to us we reject Him.

"Therefore, to you who believe, He is precious; but to those who are disobedient, The stone which the builders rejected Has become the chief cornerstone, and A stone of stumbling And a rock of offense. They stumble, being disobedient to the word, to which they also were appointed" (NKJV, 1Peter2:7&8).

God loved us (His creation) so much that He sent His Son Jesus Christ into the world to save wretched, sinful man from the penalty of death. But because of our sinful nature – due to the fall of man, we'd rather be a prisoner of sin doomed to death. You see, Jesus Christ is the very image of love and love is Jesus Christ. So, what we do is, try to find a man, woman, boy or girl to replace the ultimate love which could only be found in Jesus Christ. That is why divorce rates are on an all-time high, and people can easily get out of one marriage or relationship and jump right back into another one.

There are over 2,500 online dating services in the U.S. alone, with 1,000 new sites opening every year. Some of these dating sites charge a monthly or yearly membership fee and some offer free services.

I mean they have all kinds of sites out there - like match.com, eHarmony, Black Planet, Farmers Only, Christian Mingle, Plenty of Fish, Black People Meet, Chemistry, Over 50, Elite Singles, and gay and lesbian dating sites, just to name some. There are also reality television shows like the bachelor and bachelorette, married at first sight and love at first kiss that comes on. Can you see where we have gone wrong when it comes to "love?" I know what you may be thinking, "There is nothing wrong with going on these dating sites to find love," right? Now, am I saying these relationships from the above-mentioned dating sites will not last? No, that is not what I am saying! But, what is the probability that those relationships will last? We only hear about the success stories from these dating sites, but what about the unsuccessful stories that are not mentioned? What about the people who are married that are going on these dating websites looking to hook-up with someone? Well call me old-fashioned, but now (not that I've always known this) I believe what Proverbs 18:22 (NKJV) says, "He who finds a wife finds a good thing, And obtains favor from the Lord." I'm telling you, if someone would have instilled that in me when I was younger, I probably would not have gotten myself into some of the relationships I was in. Do I regret some of the relationships I allowed myself to get in? Sure, I do! But, I learned something new about relationships each time that shaped and molded me into the woman I am today. Most importantly, if I would not have gone through the things I went through, I would not be writing this book.

When it comes to love, no one or nothing will ever be able to measure up to the kind of love that Jesus Christ showed toward us. See, people (regardless of who they are) will disappoint you at some point in your relationship with them. But, Jesus Christ will never disappoint, mistreat, use, abandon, or cheat (to name a few) on you. The kind of love He has for us can never be duplicated! That is why you need to look to Jesus Christ for the love that you have been missing. Whether that love was missing from your childhood or in your adulthood, Jesus Christ can fill that void in your life. Then, you won't feel the need to go on all those dating sites looking for love.

I think Trip Lee said it best in his song "Looking For Love," featuring JR when he said,

You tried the pleasures of this world but still there's something missing

'Cause when you close your eyes at night you can feel your heart still searching

I know you tired of being let down so you look for love in all the wrong places

So search no more 'cause it's the life of Christ your souls been missing

When we choose to operate outside of the will of God, we set ourselves up for a life of hurt, pain, discontentment, loneliness, low self-esteem, selfishness, pride, arrogance and every other issue we wrestle with within ourselves, because of our sinful nature. Instead of waiting for love to find us, we go out and seek for it only to discover that it was not love to begin with. Then, what do we do? We start the search all over again – looking for someone else to fill that void of loneliness that we are feeling. We do not realize that at some point or another we will feel neglected or lonely in any relationship. Any time you have two people in a relationship, both parties must put in 100% effort for the relationship to work. That is why God commands us to do our part in our relationship with Him. When you have a one-sided relationship, it will not work - no matter how hard you try.

There are several reality television shows that are preying on the weakness of individuals that are "looking for love." These people that are on these reality shows are so desperate to find love that they are willing to go through extreme measures just to find love. Let's take the show Married at First Sight. The show focuses on experimental legal binding marriages facilitated by a Spiritualist (Pastor/Marriage Counselor), Psychologist, Sexologist, and Sociologist. In the show, they take six individuals (3 men and 3 women) and match them together based on their profile (opposites). They have 14 days to get married - not knowing anything about one another. They don't have any type of contact with each other until the wedding day. Here is the kicker, they don't even know each other's name. They get married, go on their honeymoon, move in together, get to know each other, and consummate the marriage if they choose. After six weeks, the couples must decide if they want to stay married or get a divorce. Although, I do not agree with the experimental marriage aspect of Married at First Sight, I do find the part in the show where the couples must get to know each other to be very important in a marriage. When people decide to date someone, I don't think they really take the time to get to know all there is to know about that person. I know I didn't! But in Married at First Sight, they have no choice but to find out EVERTHING there is to know about that person because they don't know anything about them, and they are already married. In the beginning of some relationships, people are caught up on looks, money, status, cars, houses etc. I don't believe we ask the important questions when we enter a relationship with someone. You must get to know all there is to know about a person – their mother and her family, father and his family, childhood, how many partners they have had, etc. All too often, we ignore the warning signs that that relationship is not good for us because we want to be in a relationship so bad. We will even put up with all the annoying things that person does and says in the beginning – we will even laugh at their behavior. Then overtime, what was once cute gets on our nerves and we begin to have a problem with it. If a marriage happens to take place, then you begin to uncover things about that person you didn't know or things you chose to ignore. Then, the marriage starts to go downhill and eventually ends in divorce.

Another reality show I came across (well not me, but my daughter) is called 90 Day Fiancé. In this show, US citizens meet foreigners online who live internationally and they start to date. Per the show, foreigners can enter the US on a fiancé K1-visa of American citizens. The couples have 90 days to determine whether their relationship will lead to marriage. They must get married before the 90-day visa expires or else the person must immediately return to his or her country. There are so many red flags waving and yellow blinking caution lights going off here. There are huge culture differences, language barriers, and hidden motives of those who are not US citizens that can pose major problems. Some of these people (non-US citizens) only want to get a visa so they can come to the US – while others want both a visa and money. Am I saying that the motives of all these people are deceptive? No, that is not what I'm saying. But what I am saying is, you can never fully know all there is too know about someone you meet online. Let's take 90 Day Fiancé! On one hand, you have one individual who profanes the institution of marriage for their own selfish gain. And the other person is so desperate to be married – they are totally oblivious of the intentions of their "Fiancé." If you are going to look for love online (though I don't think that is a wise decision), be very cautious because that person may not be who they say they are or who you think they are. Now, I know you may know someone who knows someone that meet their spouse online and they are living happily ever after. But, happily ever after is not always the case in every online relationship/marriage. Let's take 90 Day Happily Ever After – a follow-up of 90 Day Fiancé to show what's going on in the couple's lives. The show reveals the true intentions and character of the spouse(s). The tragedy of the whole matter is (1) they took a chance of looking for love online only to find it was more trouble than they bargained for. (2) if the marriage didn't work, they went right back online in search of finding someone else to find love – instead of learning from the first experience. I often joke about when you first meet a person, you are meeting their representative. You do not know all there is to know about that person (motives and intentions) – you only know what they want you to know or see. That is why it is extremely important to get to know everything there is to know about a person before you rush into a relationship with them. Brothers and sisters, be not easily deceived by what you see or read on the Internet or on television. Just because you received a package – wrapped in pretty paper with a red bow on it – doesn't mean you will like what's inside. Read the warning label careful – it just might say,

"Fragile, handle with care." If you are a Christian, you really don't need to be looking online for a mate (that's for free). Wait on the Lord!

We crave love because we seek to find love everywhere else except where love originated from. We look for love in people, places, things, and money; making those things our god. Deuteronomy 5:7-10 (NKJV emphasis added) states, *"You shall have <u>no other gods before Me.</u> You shall not make for yourself a carved image-any likeness of anything that is in heaven above, or that is in the earth beneath, or that is in the water under the earth; you shall not bow down to them nor serve them. <u>For I, the Lord your God, am a jealous God,</u> visiting the iniquity of the fathers upon the children to the third and fourth generations of those who hate Me, but showing mercy to thousands, to those who love Me and keep My commandments."* Love starts with and ends with God! Anything outside of that is not a 100% guarantee to last the test of time. That is why you have couples that have been married twenty plus years suddenly getting divorced. Their reason for staying married for most of those years was for the sake of the children. In today's society, people do not place any value on the institution of marriage, because they don't fully understand what marriage represents and the sacredness of it. That is why marriages are being defiled, whether heterosexually or homosexually. Oh, just so you know, whether you defile the institution of marriage heterosexually or homosexually, they both are sin and sinful.

"For there is no partiality with God. For as many as have sinned without law will also perish without law, and as many as have sinned in the law will be judged by the law. For not the hearers of the law are just in the sight of God, but the doers of the law will be justified;" (NKJV, Romans 2:11-13).

God doesn't care who you are; we will all have to give an account for everything we have ever said or done in our lives. Those who have not accepted Jesus Christ as their Lord and Savior and have not repented for their sins will not only give an account of their lives, but they will also be judged. I don't know about you, but I don't want to be sitting in the judgement seat on judgement day because I know I would be found guilty of all the accusations. When I think about it, I don't want a public defender pleading my case because public defenders are not necessarily concerned about the defendant, they are just doing their civil duty (basically their job). Oh, but I'm glad I have a lawyer that has never lost a case because ALL my sins have been paid for out on the cross at Calvary. And, I admit, I was guilty of all that I would have been accused of, but I thank God for the blood of Jesus Christ that has covered me. Now, that's enough to shout about and get my praise on!

Chapter 10

"Love Thy Neighbor"

"If someone says, I love God, and hates his brother, he is a liar; for he who does not love his brother whom he has seen, how can he love God whom he has not seen? And this commandment we have from Him: that he who loves God <u>must</u> love his brother also" *(NKJV, 1 John 4:20&21 emphasis added).*

If then, we (the body of Christ) were created in the image and likeness of God and Jesus Christ, we are to love one another. We cannot love outside of God no matter how hard we try. I'm not talking about the kind of love you have for your mother, father, siblings, spouses, children. I'm talking about loving the unlovable: loving those who mistreat you, use you, hate you, lie on you, lie to you, hurt you, stab you in the back, talk about you, slander your name, etc. Now, I know what you are thinking! How can we love people who seek to harm us? Well, God says we are to pray for those people. And not only that, we are to love them. I know that is a hard pill to swallow and it's still stuck in my throat, but in spite of how we feel about it, we must do what God has told us to do.

"No one has seen God at any time. If we love one another, God abides in us, and His love has been perfected in us" (NKJV, 1John 4:12).

What type of love do you have for others? Is it the kind of love that's based on conditions that are beneficial to you? Listen, I know it is hard to love people especially when you've been hurt over and over again. Granted, I don't know what that person has done to hurt you, but God knows. Aren't you glad about that? I am! All we have to do is stand on God's word and trust that He will work out our problems.

"Vengeance is Mine, and recompense; Their foot shall slip in due time; For the day

of their calamity is at hand, And the things to come hasten upon them" *(NKJV, Deuteronomy 32:35).*

Allow God to show you how to love, despite the situation. We've all heard this saying before: love your neighbor and hate your enemy. Well, that is not biblical. Scripture tells us, "But I say to you, love your enemies, bless those who curse you, do good to those who hate you, and pray for those who spitefully use you and persecute you. That you may be sons of your Father in heaven; for He makes His sun rise on the evil and on the good, and sends rain on the just and on the unjust" (NKJV, Matt.5:44-45). If we only love those who love us, what good is that? How would our enemies see God? If I could speak for God, (which I can't, but if I could) God is probably saying, "I see how they've treated you and they have their reward." It is so easy to love those people who treat us good and who love us back, right? Well, I hate to tell you this, but at some point, in your life you too were unlovable. Sorry, but so was I!!

One of the hardest things I had to do was love those who mistreated and used me, lied on me, slandered my name, stabbed me in the back, and hurt me. God is still working on me in that area. But, I realize that my life is not about me, but about giving God glory. And I can't give God glory if I am unwilling to love others who don't love me. I'm still under construction, *not destruction,* when it comes to loving the unlovable.

How can we <u>not</u> love someone after God loved us in spite of who we were before He saved us? He not only loves us, but He forgave us for all those sinful things we've done. Think about this! How can we expect for someone to forgive us when we've never asked that person for forgiveness? Sounds kind of crazy, right? Well, that works for God too. We must ask God for forgiveness in order to be forgiven for what we have done.

"In Him we have redemption through His blood, the forgiveness of sins, according to the riches of His grace" (NKJV, Ephesians 1:7).

Isn't that good news? That Jesus Christ who was sinless took on our sins so that we would be redeemed back to God.

Now we have access to the Father to ask for forgiveness for our sins because Jesus paid it all on the cross even though He knew we were guilty as charged. You aren't shouting yet? Excuse me, Hallelujah!

As Christians, we must forgive and love those who have wronged us. I know this can be hard to do, especially when you haven't submitted your will to the will of God. But as a Christian (child of God), our behavior should not be that of our old nature (sinful). "Love does not harm to a neighbor; therefore love is the fulfillment of the law" (NKJV, Romans 13:10). Do you not realize in order for God to forgive us of our sins, we must forgive others? Here is the kicker! If we do not forgive others for their trespasses, God will not forgive us of our trespasses. Okay, you don't believe me! "For if you forgive men their trespasses, your heavenly Father will also forgive you. But if you do not forgive men their trespasses, neither will you Father forgive your trespasses" (NKJV, Matthew 6:14-15). After all, God loved us in our mess. The victory has already been won; we just have to walk in obedience to the word of God. One thing that amazes me is how we expect God to bless us with material things, but no one wants to be obedient to the word of God. That's just crazy to me because you won't reward your child/children for being disobedient to you! But we want - excuse me, expect - God to reward us for our disobedience. Sorry to be the bearer of bad news, but God is not concerned about your material needs. He is concerned about you heart — whether you will walk in obedience to His word. Obedience is the only way you can glorify God. If you will not be obedient to the word of God, then you cannot and will not be able to please God. With that said, you cannot claim to love or know (have a relationship) God if you do not obey Him.

Here is what Jesus is telling us, "If you <u>love</u> Me, keep My commandments" (NKJV, John 14:15 emphasis added). In other words, Jesus is saying, if you do not obey what God is commanding you to do, then how can you say you love Me? I know that might be hard to accept, but that is the truth. We cannot continue to say that we love God when we won't obey what He says — it just doesn't work like that.

Prayer of Repentance

Most Gracious Heavenly Father,

You are truly worthy of all the praise, glory and honor. Lord, I come asking that You would forgive me for my sins of not being obedient to Your word. I realize that I am a sinner and I have sinned against You and You alone. Father, I confess the Lord Jesus Christ as my Savior and Lord and I believe in my heart that You raised Him from the dead. Lord, come into my heart right now! Father, thank You for loving Your creation so much that You sent Your Dearly Beloved Son, Jesus Christ, into the world to take my place out on the cross at Calvary. Jesus Christ, who knew no sin, paid the ultimate penalty of death for my sins. Thank You for raising Your Son, Jesus Christ, from the dead on the third day. Father, I know that I am not worthy, but I thank you for the blood of Jesus Christ that covered all my sins so that I would be redeemed and reconciled back to You. Lord, "Teach me to do Your will, For You are my God; Your

Spirit is good. Lead me in the land of uprightness" (NKJV, Psalms 143:10). Thank You for "open[ing] thou mine eyes that I may behold the <u>wondrous</u> things out of thy law" (KJV, Psalms 119:18 emphasis added). In Jesus Christ name I pray.

Scripture References

Genesis 1:1 (KJV)
Genesis 1:26&27 (NKJV)
Genesis 2:18&22 (KJV)
Genesis 2:20 (NKJV)
Genesis 2:24 (NKJV)
Genesis 3:1a (KJV)
Genesis 13:13 (NKJV)

Numbers 30:2 (NKJV)

Deuteronomy 5:6&7 (NKJV)
Deuteronomy 6:5 NKJV)
Deuteronomy 30:2 (NKJV)

Psalms 118:8 (NKJV)
Psalms 119:18 (KJV)
Psalms 143:10 (NKJV)

Proverbs 1:22-33 (NKJV)
Proverbs 1:26 (NKJV)
Proverbs 3:5&6 (NKJV)
Proverbs 16:1-3 (NKJV)
Proverbs 20:24 (NKJV)
Proverbs 22:6 (NKJV)
Proverbs 22:15 (KJV)
Proverbs 23:7 (NKJV)

Proverbs 23:13&14 (KJV)
Proverbs 29:15 (KJV)

Ecclesiastic 12:1 (NKJV)

Isaiah 40:31 (NKJV)
Isaiah 55:8&9 (KJV)

Jeremiah 17:19&20 (NKJV)

Matthew 5:44&45 (NKJV)
Matthew 6:19-21 (NKJV)
Matthew 6:23 (NKJV)
Matthew 6:24 (NLT)
Matthew 6:33 (NKJV)
Matthew 7:22&23 (NKJV)

Mark 3:23-27 (NKJV)

John 6:63a&b (NKJV)
John 8:7b (NKJV)

Romans 1:18 (NLT)
Romans 3:10 (NKJV)
Romans 3:23&24 (NKJV)
Romans 6:11 (NLT)
Romans 7:14-25 (KJV)
Romans 10:9 (NKJV)

1 Corinthians 6:9&10 (NKJV)

1 Corinthians 6:13-20 (NKJV)
1 Corinthians 6:18 (NKJV)
1 Corinthians 6:19 (NKJV)
1 Corinthians 7:2 (NKJV)
1 Corinthians 13:4 (KJV)
1 Corinthians 13:5&6 (NKJV)
1 Corinthians 15:33 (NKJV)

2 Corinthians 5:17 (NKJV)
2 Corinthians 6:14 (KJV)

Ephesians 1:7a (NKJV)
Ephesians 5:8 (NKJV)
Ephesians 5:11 (NKJV)
Ephesians 5:22 (NKJV)

1 Thessalonians 4:3 (NKJV)
1 Thessalonians 4:4-7 (NKJV)
1 Thessalonians 5:22&23 (NKJV)

Hebrews 13:7 (NKJV)

James 1:13&14 (NKJV)
James 1:15 (NKJV)
James 1:22&23 (NKJV)

1 Peter 1:15&16 (NKJV)
1 Peter 2:9&10 (NKJV)
1 Peter 3:1&2 (NKJV)
1 Peter 5:7 (NKJV)

2 Peter 2:21&22 (NKJV)

1 John 1:4-10 (NKJV)
1 John 2:15-17 (NKJV)
1 John 4:12 (NKJV)
1 John 4:20&21 (NKJV)
1 John 5:17 (NKJV)

Jude 1:14b&15 (NKJV)
Jude 1:16 (NLT)

Revelations 2:4 (NKJV)
Revelations 20 (NKJV)

ABOUT THE AUTHOR

Olympia Walker is a woman of God, praise dancer, wife, mother, grandmother, sister, writer, teacher, cosmetologist, and an encourager. She has a heart and passion for those who are hurting, broken and lost. Olympia knows all too well how it feels to hurt and be broken due to the lack of understanding of what true love is. She has experienced physical, mental and sexual abuse that could have destroyed her, but God had a bigger plan for her life.

Olympia wasn't "brought up in the church" as other people claim to have been. But on this Christian journey, she has realized that it does not matter if a person was "brought up in the church," or not. What's important is if that person has a relationship with God, is obedient to His word, and has accepted Jesus Christ as their Lord and Savior.